from

Other giftbooks by David Weatherson

50 Love Poems
50 Life Poems

To order additional copies of this book
call 07884 262321 or
the printers C S Podd & Son Ltd, Whyteleafe, London

My grateful thanks to my lovely wife the effervesant Susan Oliver
and my six wonderful children, Dickie, Joanne, Nancy, Sarah, David,
and young Harry, for their consistent nagging and encouragement in
the compilation of this book

Content Order

CARPENTERS CAPERS
50 verse sections about wood, sawdust & dovetails.

MECHANICS MEDALING
50 verse sections about greasy Jo & the grease monkeys.

PLUMBERS PIPES
50 verse sections about pots, pipes & pandimonium.

THE SOLE PUPOSE OF THIS BOOK IS TO

GIVE PEOPLE AN EXCUSE TO LAUGH OUT

LOUD AND SHOW THEIR FEELINGS. WITH

SO MUCH STRIFE AND MISERY AROUND

THIS WORLD, LETS ALL HAVE FUN AND SEE

THE LIGHTER SIDE OF TRADESMEN.

Carpenters Poems

01.
My husband is a carpenter, he makes things out of wood'
He made some lovely chairs last week, they really were quite good.
The wood was teak, he kept the streak, with butts and dovetails too,
Then wrapped them up all pretty and said here wife, their for you.

02.
My old mans a chippie, he works the building sites,
To make that extra money, he's turned to working nights,
But as I get quite cold at night, Iv taken in a lodger,
He's six foot two, with eyes of blue, his name is Jammy
Dodga.

03.

When at school I played the fool, and couldn't grasp the lessons,
My teachers and my parents put it down to adolescence,
I failed exams and got reports of comments like "too lippy",
So 14 came and I left school apprenticed to a chippie.

I really felt at ease with this, and helped to make a sofa,
Just to prove to one and all, that this boy is no loafer,
Second week I made some pegs, then fixed a broken table,
Then I made a back-yard broom, for my dear Auntie Mabel.

As years went by I did my time, with 5 year as apprentice,
It took my brother 7 years, as he is now a dentist,
The moral is no matter what, doctor, sparks, or smithy,
Stick to what you shine at best, in my case it was chippie.

04.

Carpenter, Carpenter make me a seat, I need to sit down
and rest my poor feet,

Iv walked the world over from Barnsley to Crete, But never
been able to find a good seat,

Iv sat down on wood, and Iv sat down on stone, Iv sat
down abroad and Iv sat down at home,

Iv sat on a chair and on a settee, but never have found a seat
to suit me.

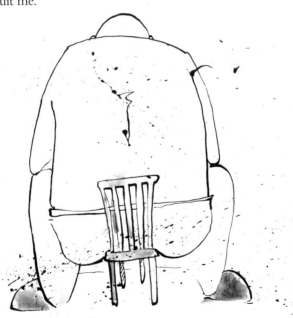

05.

Chippies work with wood and nails, G Clamps, plains, and hammers,
They work on site they swear and spit, they really have no manners,
And at days end when work is done, and overalls are off,
They rush straight home, grab knife and fork, their teas to fiercely scoff,

It's then straight in to easy chair, and focused on the telly,
With control pad in the left hand, and a beer propped on his belly,
At half past eight he falls asleep, and into bed for ten, then up next day for half past six, to start it all again.

06.

A carpenter got sick one day, he slipped and hurt his back,
His mate took him to hospital, and said it's my mate Jack,
The doctor said I,ll take a look, his backs all bruised and peeling,
The mate said yes, I'm not surprised; he fell right through the ceiling.

07.

A chippie once was banging nails, when oops he hit his thumb,
He said oh look its gone all blue, and feeling rather numb,
He jumped around and had a swear, the air turned really blue,
And then he said be careful lads this could occur to you.

08.
Carpenters wear little bags, all tied around their waist,
The purpose is to carry nails, and cut down on the waste,
There's slots to put the hammer the chisel and the cleats,
Theyve even got a zipper to keep a few nice sweets.

There's places for the wood saw, the plumb-bob, and some
rags,
Theyve even made a little slot, to fit a pack of fags,
Allowing for the tools and things, this bag will be quite
heavy,
But never fear there's always space to fit a lunch time
bevvey.

09.
Carpenters from Manchester, and Carpenters from Stoke,
Carpenters who take a drink, and Carpenters who smoke,
Carpenters from Bromley, way down in sunny Kent,
Carpenters who're on the straight, and Carpenters who're
bent,
Carpenters who're rather short, and Carpenters who're tall,
Carpenters who go to church, oh Good Lord bless them all.

10.
My cousin was a chippie and made a lot of money,
My uncle was a circus clown and really rather funny,
My sister was a papal nun, and wore a long black habit,
My brother a magician, with big top hat and rabbit.

11.

I work down at the saw-mills, with all the dust and noise,
I'm 6ft 5 and 18 stone, a big man with the boys,
When more big trees are needed they call the lumberjack,
Thats when I save them time and cash, I bring them on my
back.

I pick them up and set them down, exactly where there
needed,
I even cultivate the ground, and leave it all re-seeded,
I'm really such a handsome chap, and always in demand,
Iv even got the village girls eating out my hand,

I really like my strong physique, my muscles and my body,
It makes up for my silly name, it starts with N, its Noddy.

12.

C is for Carpenter gifted and good
A is for Artisan working with wood
R is for Reggie the Carpenters name
P is the smoother and that's called the Plane
E is for edges all rubbed down and soft
N is for night owl, up in the loft
T is for Tennon–Saw carpenter's friend
E is for ecstasy at the job end
R is for rubbing to polish the wood
S is for sales, and that makes you feel good

13.
Most Chippies now are single lads, working on new houses,
Looking down on girls below, wearing skimpy blouses.

14.
Chippies, Joiners, Carpenters, what is in a name,
They,ve all got wood in common, running through a vein,
They,ve all got blackened thumb-nails and saw dust in their hair,
Chippies all wear bib and brace, you'll spot them anywhere.

15.

Chippies chip, and Joiners join, do carpenters lay carpets?
Squadies march by left and right, mechanics work in car-
pits,
Farmer's farm, and racers race, do dustmen carry dust?
Of course they don't you silly chap, do sailors die of rust?

16.

We got a quote to fix the hall, as all the roof was rotten,
The rain came in, the floor was wet, the carpets truly
sodden,
Joiner Bill was cheapest quote, just under 15 thou,
He said for cash I,ll work at night, Il even start right now.

17.

I'm 18 stone and 6ft 3, and weaned on Craster Kippers,
We got through 6 pr every day, the wife and our four
nippers,
We chew the bones, and suck the skin, but throw away the
head,
Then as that sweet smell lingers, we all go off to bed,

You may well ask what relevance this story has on wood,
Well none for me, my dads at sea, and Id go if I could,
But I'm too fat to go to sea, Id drown and loose my life,
Il stay a big fat carpenter, with my four kids and wife.

18.

There's two by four, and six by eight, and three inch
wooded dowels,
There's three-eighths screws, and six inch nails,
And two foot rails for towels
Block hammers come in quarter pound, and this all sounds
like sums,
As when you ask for nuts and bolts, they come in kilo
drums.

19.

I made a Kist, I made a chair, a box from solid pine,
To make a stool was quite a breeze, I made not one but 9,
I then branched out to furniture, a bed a big welsh dresser,
A dolls house for my little girl, she thinks I'm tops, oh bless
her,

A desk a bench a garden hutch, for chickens and pet mice,
I once carved out an animal, now that was really nice,
I made a hedge, an ocean ship, a house with all its ribbing,
Oh what the heck, it's all made up, you know I'm only
kidding.

20.
Archie is a carpenter who works with oak and teak,
You'll know he comes from Scotland when you hear him
start to speak,
Its och I this, and hoots the noo, and other Scottish verse,
But when he's had a drink or two, believe you me, its worse.

21.

A joiner punched his boss one day, right between the eyes,
He told his wife, that geek at work, I,v punched his two
mince pies,
She said you're such a silly chap, whatever was the cause,
He said because my beard was white he called me Santa
clause,

The wife said you're too easily riled; you must control your
temper,
Just stick to words, and call him dog, and hope he gets
distemper,
The joiner thought this rather cute and planned his deed all
week,
He sent him an exploding bone, to Fido Mr Geek!

22.
Andy was a joiner boy, who worked near Bolams mill,
And if your ever Alnwick way, you'll see it stands there still,
Although the mill is standing there, sadly Andy's not,
A yield sign into Fenkle St, old Andy overshot.

23.

Joiner Jack he had a dog, it was his friend and pet,
So when the mutt got sick one day, he telephoned the vet,
He said oh vet I'm quite concerned, whatever could it be,
Bring him in the vet replied, lets see what we can see,

The dog was groaning, panting fast, could hardly walk a yard,
The vet he pressed, then did some tests, then said his guts feel
hard,
Il have to do some x-rays now, this all seems rather weird,
And then he said, look there it is, its all just as Iv feared,

Inside the dog was nuts and bolts, screws and joiners tape,
Everything was food to him, nothing did escape,
You see the dog had learnt from birth, to clean behind his
master,
Instead of brushing up the bits, he'd eat it, it was faster.

24.

A carpenter he bought a bike to keep in peak condition,
To ride it more than half a mile he found it quite a mission,
His hat blew off his specs fogged up, and then he lost his
way,
He thought well blow this for a laugh, and threw the bike
away.

25.

The carpenter came round today to build my Mum a
bench,
And as he walked inside the room, we thought pew, what's
that stench,
He'd stepped right in some doggy doo while walking in the
street,
And now he'd spread it on the rug, as it was on his feet.

My Mum said oi you dirty man, please take off your shoes,
Id saved so hard to buy that rug, you've given me the blues,
Il cheer you up said chippie, a deal you'll get from me,
In fact to try and make amends, Il build the bench for free.

26.
I often thought a carpenter was strange, or odd, or queer,
He'd always have a pencil stub, lodged behind his ear,
It wouldn't be a normal one, long with plenty lead,
But rather just a short fat shape, flat against his head.

27.

A chippie saved his sawdust up, and filled bags to the top,
He'd sell it to the butcher to sprinkle in his shop,
It soaked up all the blood and muck, and kept things looking neat,
And meant you didn't slip and slide, and felt good under feet.

Then came along the council with much aplomb and show,
And said were part of Europe now, the sawdust has to go,
The chippie herd the butchers plight and came right to his aid,
Not because he liked the man, but caus he'd not been paid.

The butcher said it's not your fault,
And paid him from his bureau,
Instead of paying 20 quid, he paid him 20 Euro,
Don't bring the sawdust round no more, but carry on with logs,
And don't blame me or council staff, its Europe and the frogs.

28.

I knew a Scottish carpenter who lives up in the Glen,
Where boys are boys, and girls are girls, and men are really
men,
They wake at six to chop the sticks and wash in freezing
waters,
Then men they work, boys they fish, and cleanings done by
daughters.

29.

My dad knew Fishy Woodman, who lived down by the sea
He'd sit and tell me all these tales while we were having tea,
Now Fishy had a two ton van, a Morris Model T,
Then him and dad would tootle off on Fridays after tea,
They first would back into a field then fill the van with
spuds,
Then turnips by the dozen with loads of heavy thuds.

How they'd never been found out was really quite a fluke,
As all in all their stealings were really from the Duke,
Oh why did Fishy do these things was nicking so inbred,
No it was sawdust there in place of brains in Fishy
Woodman's head.

30.

Eddie Bow the joiner bought a monkey for a pet,
He said come on lets get you checked, were off to see the vet,
The monkey ahhd, and showed his teeth, and widdled in a jar,
But then when asked to touch his toes, said stop you've gone too far.

I know you see me as your pet, and think I'm rather funny,
But if you think I play those games, think again there sonny,
Young Eddie said you've got it wrong, were not such filthy scum,
Wed rather work from morn till night than see your dirty bum.

31.

I'm a joiner I'm a carpenter I make things out of wood,
Although I blow my trumpet loud I'm really rather good,
I make things for the trendy folk, to laugh at ha, ha, ha,
I make things for the export trade, my business stretches far,

Iv got a branch in Canada, and even Istanbul,
Got offices in London, and a sub branch up in Hull,
Got partners out in Paris, and a dealer out in Bream,
Oh pinch me please and wake me from this tantalizing
dream.

32.

Kipper was the wood-yard cat who slept out in the shed,
With clothes to keep the draught out, and sawdust for his
bed
Late at night a friend would come his name was Maurice
Mouse,
He'd say to Kip, come on old son I'm off into the house,

Together they would sneak inside and suss out all the food,
Said Kipper cat to Maurice Mouse, this all seems rather
good,
I think well find a place to hide and make this place our
home,
Said Maurice Mouse to Kipper cat, don't leave me hear
alone,

They set up house and lived as one, the owners non the
wiser,
They ate the steak, and chewed the chops, they even drank
the Tizer,
So no more draughty shed with sawdust for his pillow,
He's got the latest cat-size bed, made out of finest willow.

33.

The joiners wife had wind one night, it really was quite
smelly,
It came from deep within her loins, inside her big fat belly,
She said oh please excuse me chuck, it must have been the
tart,
Now every time I cough or sneeze, I do a little fart,

All that night she belched and blew, and farted without
thinking,
When morning came her husband said you really are quite
stinking,
My love she said I'm deeply shocked I don't know what's the
matter,
Then bending forward elbows
raised, she farted what a clatter,

He said that's it you filthy hag,
your fartings gone too far,
Just change your smelly underpants
and meet me at the car,
I'm taking you to see the doc,
a remedy to find,
I hope he has a giant cork to wedge
up your behind.

34.
Joiners dogs are small and loud, quite uncouth and brassy,
and all have common back-street names like, Jip, and Rex,
and Lassie.

35.

The joiner and his missus went to town on Friday night,
The joiner said oh wifie you look a pretty site,
Your hair is looking lovely and your eyes are shinning
bright,
And your teeth are like the stars above, they come out every
night.

36.

What has teeth but doesn't bite?, a saw I hear you say,
What has whistles but no tune?, steam trains in my day,
What has keys but plays no song? a jailer in the nick,
And what has sand but got no beach, a sandwich, nice and
thick.

37.

Have a nice day chippie, the sun is shinning bright,
You're working in fresh air today, your flooring out on site,
You've got your trusty thermos, and your sarnies nice and thick
Now bend your back and push the job, you'll find it goes quite quick.

38.
There was an old joiner from Crew,
Who managed to turn the air blue,
He'd spit and he'd swear, and he'd pull out his hair,
And end up in a terrible stew.

39.

The carpenter arrived on site but couldn't find his tools,
He said I blame those sparky chaps they are a bunch of
fools,
Last week they took the toilet seat, removed it clean off site,
Now my joiners bum gets cold when going for a sh——.

They nicked the foreman's safety boots and filled them with
cement,
And then said come on take a joke, you know there's no
harm meant,
But he was having none of it, and threw them off the job,
So its good-bye to Jack and Sam, and Scottish stinky Bob.

40.

Welshman Pete had stinky feet, when walking up the ladder,
But what was worse was Ronnie Hurs, who had a leaky
bladder.

41.

Sitting in Northumberland deep amongst the hills,
With clean fresh air and mountain streams, and curlews piercing shrills,
Looking out to Kielder, a forest standing proud,
All you hear is quietness, quietness so loud,
Miles and miles of slender trees, isn't it a pity,
That one day they'll be felled and sold, to serve wood to the chippie.

42.

The chippies wife was Susan a buxom country lass,
Who liked to see the big world from the bottom of a glass,
She liked a drink of whisky, and she liked a drink of gin,
And you knew when she was ticking by that alcoholic grin,

But poor old chippie paid the price, when Sue was drinking late,
He'd get to work with frozen chips, and ice pops for his bait,
He said now Sue I love you dear, but drinking's got to stop,
Or else Il leave for foreign parts with easy jet non stop,
She begged don't go, Il change my ways, the booze wont rule my life,
Il loose 5 pound and learn to cook, Il be the perfect wife.

43.

Isabel looked rather swell, a tall and stunning looker,
Rumor has it days gone by, she used to be a hooker,
But now she's changed and settled down, no more the
trendy hippie,
She's married peace in rural life, and married Ken the
chippie.

44.
The carpenter is sick today, its something that he ate,
It could be all that beacon, that was pilled up on his plate,
You see he had the special that was beacon, egg, and chips,
And now he's lying groaning saying, nothing past my lips.

45.

Bill went off to night school, a carpenter to be,
He said its great Iv fancied this right from the age of three,
They taught him all the angles, of dove tail, and tech
drawing,
They even taught him how to stand when doing simple
sawing,

He learnt of all the measurements, of inch, and foot, and
yard,
And then they started metric, but Billy found this hard,
He said Il choose imperial to measure for my work,
For if I go the metric route Il really look a burk,

The teacher said OK young Bill, the choice is really yours,
Now for your test Id like to see a set of cupboard doors,
Later on with doors complete the pace had been quite
hectic,
Young Billy had surpassed himself, he'd done it all in metric.

46.

The local hag from down the street was called old Sally Straker,

She shocked the town on old years night and wed the cabinet maker,

Her hair was lank, her teeth were brown, her breath was foul and stinking,

And all her man could do was stare, while petrified and blinking,

He knew he'd made a big mistake, but fear had kept him going,

But what he'd got planned in his head, well only he was knowing.

47.

My name is Jess and I'm a dog, my master is a joiner,
We packed our bags and headed for the island of Iona,
He takes me with for company, for friendship and support,
The deal is I can sleep the trips, but wake up when in port,

I'm welcome in the hotel and even in the bar,
I'm tolerated poolside and often in the car,
They draw the line at meal times and bar me from the
lounge,
That's when I'm in the kitchens sniffing on the scrounge.

48.

Joiners live in wooden houses, eat off wooden tables,
They sit on polished wooden chairs and tell their children
fables.

49.

Some joiners go to work in Fords, some bosses go in Jags,
Some joiners turn up neatly dressed, while some pitch up in
rags,
Some joiners keep their tool box neat, and keep their vans
real tidy,
Some joiners clean on Saturdays, while others plumb for
Friday.

50.

Some joiners drink, some joiners smoke, some joiners even gamble,

Some joiners like the week-end break and take off on a ramble,

Some joiners they play cricket, and quite a few play soccer,

While one or two like chasing birds, now isn't that a shocker.

Mechanics Poems

01.

Mechanics are a dirty lot, with hands all black and smelly
With oil and grease and petrol stains, all smeared across their belly,
They wear big boots all smeared in gunge, and don't walk straight, they tend to lunge.
They all drink milk with Big Joe pies, and all have stains around their flyes
Their skin is white and faces spotty; their lifestyle really is quite grotty.

02.

I took my car to get it fixed it really was appauling,
As I was driving down the street I'd hear the locals calling
Hey what's the make, a scrap yard car?, hope you're not
planning driving far
The door was bent the light was broke, the cable snapped
for manual choke.

I rolled into the garage yard and asked to see the foreman
He said good-day how can I help, my name is honest
Norman
I said I need the car fixed up and moneys not a worry
I'll leave it with you for a while, I'm really in no hurry

Then Norman took a walk around, and pulled, and pushed,
and poked
He said it's in an awful state, he sniggered and he joked
I said you've really got me cross, it's my trusted Austin Maxi
Now take your garage and your jokes, and stick them up
your jacksie!.

03.

Mike the mechanic was working one day
When a catchy wee tune just wafted his way
He hummed and he tapped, and he whistled and sang
The start of his pop group went off with a bang

Slowly but surely his mates all joined in
All on their "instruments" gosh what a din
with Lennie on spanners and old Reg to hum
Jim on car bonnet, converted to drum

Jack on the air pipe and Tim on the saw
The foreman on whistle commanding the floor
The girls from the switchboard joined in with their backings
Then in walked the big boss, and started the sackings

04.
Mechanics from Ireland, mechanics from Nice
mechanics all smelly and covered in Grease

05.

Mechanics work in garages, all sheltered from the sun,
their skins all white and milky, they never have much fun,
but come the summer holidays, their off to sunny Spain,
leaving all that Pommey cold, the damp the fog, the rain.

Their little white legs sticking out, from underneath their
belly
They look just like a snow-drop, wobbling like jelly,
They whoop it up, and knock it back, the finance they don't
panic
They'll square it up with overtime, employed as a mechanic.

06.
Mechanics work in boiler suits, and some they wear a cap,
The reason for the boiler suite, to hide the old butt-gap.

07.
Mechanics they are grease monkeys by any other name,
Fixing cars and trucks and vans, is their daily game,
They'll change the oil, and fix the brakes, and then adjust the tappets,
Then if the vehicle's past its best, they'll just suggest you scrap it.

08.

Working in a garage you get to play with toys,

There's the quiet slinky car lifts, the wheel brace with its noise,

The automatic greaser and the clicking of the wrench,

with the mechie banging madly at the brake shoes on the bench.

With the quiet balancing of the wheels with just a quiet hum,

To the setting of the tappets, banging like a drum.

09.

Mechanics come from Birmingham, mechanics come from
Crew
Mechanics can be anybody, even me and you
Mechanics who have worked their time and rose up to the
top,
And mechanics who prefer the grease stay firmly in the shop,
Mechanics come from Inverness, and Heddon-On-The-Wall
Mechanics keep us running smooth, that's why we bless them
all.

10.
Mechanics that's black, mechanics that's pink,
Mechanics that sweat, mechanics that stink.

11.

My brother is a mechie, he works the whole day through.
My sister is a copper and works from 6 till 2.
My brothers happy fixing cars, dressed scruffy in his clobber.
My sister she's real happy too, when trying to catch the
robber.

12.

To fault an engines automated, diagnosed with ease.
No more crouching in the dirt, kneeling on your knees.
All you do is plug it in, and flick those magic knobs.
In fact it does the tests itself, while you do other jobs.

13.

My father knew a techie, foreman was his rank.
He used to come and visit us, we lived at Hefla bank.
He used to come with Dixon the gaffer of the place.
A big tall man, a handsome chap, with patch upon his face.
He wore the patch to signify he only had one eye.
But is seemed to do him little harm, he wed a girl called Vi.

14.
Some mechanics work on cars, and some they work on ships.
For some they get a hefty pay, while some rely on tips.
Some work on the barges, while some work out at sea.
Some work up in Lockerby, and some in Peterlee.

15.

I knew a techie with the runs, he really had the skitter.
I think it came from carrot juice; his aim was to get fitter.
He lifted weights, he chewed his greens, he did it all for fun.
But every time he broke his wind, the toilet he did run.

He thought no wait this is no joke.
I really hate this runs thing.
As now I've wiped my bum so much.
Iv ended up with ring-sting.

16.
Techies have dogs, and techies have kittens.
Techies in winter wear thick wooly mittens.

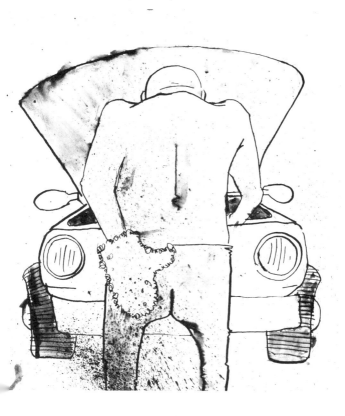

17.
Some techies are black, some techies are white.
Some techies are greedy and work every night.

18.

Bill was a mechanic who lived way down in Wales.
Now Bill could hold you captive with all his garage tales.
He told a story after tea, it ran into the night.
The end result was all the children, wet the bed with fright.

The mums they all chastised old Bill.
And said you should know better.
At this the children laughed some more.
And made the bed more wetter.

I think you ought to leave us now.
Said mother to old Bill.
And as she pushed him out the door.
Jokes he was telling still.

He shouted through the letter box.
I only need a minute.
To crack this joke and make you laugh.
The room and all those in it.

19.
Nancy was a techie, a strange job for a lady.
She said it doesn't worry me, my foreman's name is Sadie.

20.
I am a gay mechanic, and I live down by the sea.
Brighton is my stomping ground, thats where I feel so free.
So free to really be myself, to jump, and sing, and shout.
And when I run along the beach, my willies hanging out.

We swim and frolic in the sea, and always sunbathe nude,
And people who don't share my views, they really think I'm rude.
But back at work I'm Gregory, the homosexual techie,
Where all the boys laugh at my skirt and call me Lady Becky.

21.

I know a jolly techie who likes his steak and chips,
He likes it just a bit too much, as noticed by his hips.
He starts to wheeze and can't bend down to get beneath a car,
And as his chest is 40B he has to wear a bra.

22.

I knew a fat mechanic, who really loved to eat,
His eyes were big, his guts were big, as was his giant feet.
Arms the size of tree-trunks, his nose was like a carrot,
He lived at No, 28, his name was fatty Jarrot.

Breakfast time was big Jack pies, three to be precise.
Washed down with a quart of milk, laced with blocks of ice.
Lunch time was a poke of chips, with three large hake and
batter.
And as he scoffed the food with ease, his belly just got fatter.

23.
I knew an ex mechanic chap, who never made the grade.
He'd start off well and study hard, but gradually he'd fade.
He tried to do some night school, and concentrate on
theory,
But this fell flat, he missed his mates, and told the school
"I'm weary".

He thought I know, I'll learn by post, and do the course at
home,
I'll have my folks to help me through, and I'll not feel alone.
But this fell through come summer time, he started playing
cricket,
And to this day, that ex mechanic's still a raging thicket.

24.
Iv got to do an interview, as I'm the garage foreman,
Iv got this chap at 2.15, his name is Archie Norman.
He comes with good credentials, he seems to know his
stuff, but as you know at interviews, it's easy for to bluff.

I know what I'll get him on, the theory of compression,
And as I know the answers I'll make a good impression.
He'll really think I'm on the ball, and give me huge respect,
He'll work so hard and make me rich, then everything's
perfect.

25.
Roly Dean from Rochester wakes up each day at five,
Has a shave, two cups of tea, then off to work he'll drive.
He gets down to the garage and parks his car for six,
He boils the kettle, warms the pot, then has more tea and
bicks.

26.
Billy Gibson's father had a lovely way with words,
While Billy Gibson junior could really pull the birds.
Between the two they worked real hard and built a thriving trade,
Cars, and vans, and motorbikes, they really had it made.

Younger Bill would get the work by dishing out the patter,
Young girls, old girls, granny's, it really didn't matter.
Then old Bill said your cars aren't safe, they need some brand new parts,
The Gibson coffers need topped up, pay up you hags and tarts.

27.

My friend he runs a garage shop, up North in Peterlee,
A lovely little tourist place, not too far from the sea.
He sells his nuts and bolts quite well, and loads of different oils,
With spark plugs, belts, and dynamos, wiper blades and coils.

He's now branched into overalls, protective shoes and caps,
When all togged out from head to toe, the techies look smart chaps.
But with the job comes dirt and grime, grease and oil and sweat,
Then Friday night its one job lot, straight to the launderette.

28.

I know a queer mechanic, his day time name is Burt,
Come evening time he hits the clubs, his stage name being
Girt.
He squeezes into women's clothes, stockings with high heels,
Then as the MC calls his name, he's clapped on stage midst
squeals.

He sings his songs and tells his jokes, while lapping up the
praise,
And when he tells the raunchy ones the roof old Girt can
raise.
He then concludes his raunchy show by singing hits by
Queen,
That being what he is by night, an undercover queen.

29.

Dougie Brown was super fit, swimming weights, and running,
You'd see him lifting up small cars his strength was really stunning.
The girls would come from miles around, to see this local hero,
When asked what gave him all his strength, he said pies made with Be-Ro.

30.

M is for Morris a car to fix up.

E is for Engine petrol to supp.

C is for carb, where petrol runs through.

H is for heater, so we don't turn blue.

A is for Austin a fine English car.

N is for number plate, 8 AJR.

I is for Inlet, a hard working valve.

C is for Charlie, the owner from Garve.

31.
A Black man came from Africa to learn the garage trade,
A white man came from Aberdeen, in used cars for to trade.
A yellow man from China came to buy a car with rice,
A brown girl came from Swaziland, now she was rather nice.

32.

When still at school in 62, my teacher said to me,
Come on son, let's think out loud, what would you like to be.
You're almost at the age to leave, and start your chosen trade,
The last thing that you need to do, is just sit back and fade.

I thought you know, this buggers right, I mustn't really panic,
And as I like fast cars and noise Il be a race mechanic.
I see my life ahead of me, success fine wine and women,
With lazy days, and party nights, and plenty bare-buff
swimming.

But at this point my bubble burst, the school bell rang for
lunch,
Id come back to reality with one almighty punch.
The nearest I'll get to a car is cleaning with a shammy,
Unless I win the Ernie Bonds, and that would be real jammy.

33.

The boy stood on the burning deck, frozen stiff with panic,
His father hard at work below, he was a trained mechanic.
He yelled fear not my frightened son, Id never let you burn,
Iv almost got the sprinklers fixed, then this big wheel Il turn.

He shouted out I'll save you all, I'll even save the ship,
Then P and O will pay me, with a round the world free trip.
But at this point his nightmare stopped, he sat upright in bed,
And said oh wife I had this dream and all I saw was red.

She said that wasn't flames you saw, you drunken silly fool,
Look what you've done to our dear son, he's lying in a pool.
You've covered him with water, by emptying the jug,
Then zonked him with my dentures as you emptied out my
mug.

34.
Car bus, truck, or van,
You need a mechanic, I'm your man.
Boat plane, train, or yacht,
How to fix them, I know not.

35.

I'm Harry Hogg from Hudersfield, hello, how do you do,
Oh hi I'm Kie, Iv just arrived, I come from Katmandu.
The third one said hello I'm Fred and I'm from Inverness,
Then came a man from Warrington, who said his name was
Press.

They'd come for a convention, a three day seminar,
Local lads and foreigners, who'd really traveled far.
Theyd talk crank shafts in the morning, pistons after lunch,
Then tappets in the evening, a dedicated bunch.

36.

Norman was a naturist who loved to sunbathe nude,
His next door neighbors scorned his ways, and called him
vial and rude.
They said now come on Norman, haven't you got shame,
Clean up your act, behave yourself, and try to play the
game.

If tanning nude you think was bad, well just imagine work,
He'd fix his engines starkers, well really what a burke.
With oil and grease on back and front, he really looked
quite silly,
And yes you've guessed it, all his keys, were hanging on his
willey!.

37.

I used to work in garages, but now Iv been promoted,
No more greasy overalls, no more dirty coated.
I'm in the show-room selling cars, trailers, vans, and
campers,
And if I meet my target, I scoop the month end hampers.

Everyone's got money, ready cash or cheques,
I even serve celebrities, Loo Loo, Posh and Becks.
I test drive all the latest cars, and go to all the doo,s,
And with this top-end glamour job, I never get the blues.

38.
I bought a Morris Minor, it cost me 50 quid
When I picked up my kids from school, they all ran off and hid.
They said Dad this old banger is not the car for us,
Unless you buy a newer one, well have to catch the bus.
They said I'd failed, why weren't we rich, like good old Uncle Tony,
I said that's it, from hear on in, you go on Shank's Pony.

39.
M for Morris, J for Jag,
S for Skoda, what a drag,
R for Roller, M for Merc,
I've a Vauxhall, what a burke.

40.

Why aren't girls mechanics, working under cars,
An ideal place to keep their tools would be inside their bras.
Their big long nails could turn the screws, their high heels,
that's a hammer.
Imagine in the workshop, what a place of glamour.
Instead of on the garage wall, all those girlie stickers,
You'd have the real thing walking round, in frilly bra's and
knickers.

41.

One eyed Dave's the foreman, Willies on the tyres,
Dixon's going round the farms, doing deals in Byers.
Maurice serving petrol, and Cookie serving grease,
With George Cooke chief mechanic, accounts was Annalise.

The church is now a car park, and Dixon sadly gone,
But Stewie and young David will keep the business on.
The businesses yes its Blackshaws, senonoumus with
Alnwick,
Famous for its service and stature of mechanic.

42.

I'm a techie with a difference, as I work down on the farm,
I'm really rather passive, and would do a fly no harm.
I never tighten belts too much, in case I make them squeak,
And when I take old tires off, to them I try to speak.

I tell them not to worry, I'll never burn them down,
Instead they go to children, to bowl around the town.
I never use a hammer, and don't adjust the clutch,
I'm a passive old mechanic, with a very gentle touch.

43.

I've bent oil in my foo foo valve, whatever can I do,
The car went bang, and sparks flew out, a mouse ran out the floo.
A fish was in the water hose, a ferret in the sump,
Jack-daws nesting in the boot, a frog stuck in the pump.
I lifted up the bonnet and to my great surprise,
Two sheep were playing chop-sticks before my very eyes.

44.
Mini car, stretch car, racing car, more,
If I add cable car, then I have four.

45.

Billy Smails from Chatterton woke up with such a fright,
I can't remember where I parked, I had a drink last night.
I have a clear cut vision of driving to the pub,
As Jack the German shepherd, he pittled on my hub.

He pittled on the bumper then he pittled on the door,
When I got out the dog jumped in, and pittled on the floor.
He pittled on the steering wheel and pittled on the dash,
On anything that didn't move, that dog would have a slash.

I thought OK he's empty now he surely has to stop,
But as I pulled him from the car, he did a further drop.
It landed on the driving seat, the place I have to sit,
And as he landed on the ground, on my shoes he shit.

I said that's it you filthy mutt, your owner has to pay,
Until he does the pub car park is where my car will stay.

46.

Susan was a special girl who bought a brand new car,
She said I need a sporty job, I need to travel far.
My jobs in the community, caring for the old,
So give me special pricing please, if I may be so bold.

The salesman said don't worry Sue, I once was a mechanic,
A good sound car is what you'll get so please now, don't
you panic.
I'll give it to you less 15, and if this deal is made,
I'll take your old existing honk, in part exchange for trade.

Said Susan listen hear young chap you don't dictate to me,
I always get my way in life, that's how it's meant to be.
I'm the youngest of a brood of 6, and always had my say,
Start talking sense and cut a deal, or else I'll walk away.

At this the chap got worried and didn't want to loose,
OK he said, less 25, and colour you can choose.
That's better said young Susan, tape?, CD?, and mags?,
Oh as I like to shop a lot, I,ll need a rack for bags.

101

47.

When you're next up Scunthorpe way, allow two extra hours,
Call in to 16 Icomm St, you'll know it by the flowers.
For there's a chap called Skippy Brown, who works on cars for days,
He covers them with artwork, a wild and scented haze.
Tulips on the windows, daisy's on the roof,
Pansies on the aerial, I think young Skips a poof.

He really does a work of art, he's every bit a pro,
An artist by profession, he always gives a show.
Now if these flowers aren't for you, and get you misconstrued,
Just drop him 50 extra quid, he does a crackin nude!.

48.

Am a Geordie lad from Newcastle, a Magpie through and through,

A joined Sir Bobby's army at the tender age of 2.

A gan tiv all the matches and join in all the songs,

Winter time all still be there wearing warm lang-Johns.

49.

I like a pint of bitter after all the graft of day,
And as for naughty G and T,s I sure can put away.
I'll take a port and lemon, and I'm partial to a pimms,
But let me loose on vodka and I develop rubber limbs.

I'm a devil on the whisky and get plastered on the sherry,
And as for port and cooking wine, that really gets me merry.
Brandy makes me randy and that's the age old rhyme,
And what I hate the most in life, the barman shouting time.

Now this drinking ,s not a habit, not a drop all through the
week,
I'm far too busy fixing cars, the rattle and the squeak.
Yes through the weeks for working, for overtime and cash,
Then Friday night I start again, my normal week-end bash.

104

50.

Tiny Tim from Tonbridge Wells, never baths and often smells,
His hair is long a sheer disgrace, with spots and chorbs upon
his face.
His teeth are yellow never clean, he won't by soap he's far too
mean.

His ears are full of wax and muck, he really is a filthy shmuck,
But having said these horrid things, oh by the way he wears
nose rings.
He really studied well at school, and never once did act the
fool,
This top mechanic turned out well, pity about the awful
smell.

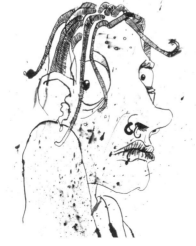

Plumbers Poems

01.
The plumber bent to fix the tap
And all we saw was his butt gap
The more he bent the more we saw
With nosy naighbours at the door

Word had spread right up the road
On what on us he had bestowed
He banged and sawed to get it right
Ah what a noise, oh what a sight.

02.

Plumbers tools are not well known
Because their names are seldome shown
Theres mole-wrench, rasps, and rodding sticks
Names more like magicians tricks
But if you think these bring a smile
What about the "bastard file"
Theres rude names too like "blow-torch" "flux"
That's sure to get discerning looks
With "stilstons" "jack saws" "plumbers putty"
These names will surley drive you nutty

03.

The names a plumber gives his firm
Would surley make a teacher squirm
Theres jones the "plummer" day or "nite"
Call for "leek" and get it "rite"
Theres "mr mole-grip" never fails
With "cach" your drips in moffats "pails"

04.

Plumbers of the world unite
Lets hope we get called out tonight
Double time with lots of lolly
All the plumbers rich and jolly

05.

The pipe has burst the water leaks, its pouring down the ceiling
The thought of getting all new things is really quite appealing
Ill let it run a little more before i call the plumber
Theres no big rush and anyway, i think ive lost his number
Next day comes, the plumbers been, and now comes the assessor
She writes a cheque for 20 grand, oh thanks a lot, oh bless her.

06.

The plumber wakes on fathers day
The telephones switched off
His wife has put it out of reach
Its hidden in the loft

She says your staying here today
To rest and just relax
He says my love im missing jobs
There cash i,l pay no tax

But family ties are stronger
And his wife stays in the shed
And jeff the plumber stays at home
Relaxing in his bed

07.

Pete the plumber,s off to work
Merry as he goes
But as he was so drunk last night
He,s gone without his clothes

08.
The plumbers got a call out
It comes from Dr hurst
He rubs his hands with joy and glee
Hes off to fix a burst

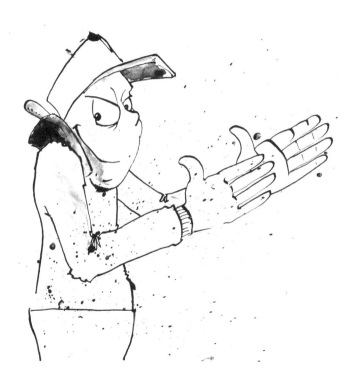

09.

The waters pouring through the floor
The customer is desporate
He says ill pay you 50 quid
And keep the tax bill separate

Its cash in hand
Not through the books
Streight to the old sky rocket
Just come right now with all your tools
Your stilstons, mole, and socket

10.

A lady plumber came to us, she really was apealing
But after only half a day, her foot came through the ceiling
She dropped the hammer on the cat, and frightend off the parrot
And then to fix a leaking tap she used a mouldy carrot
She really didn't have a clue and did more harm than good
What started out to be a drip, turned out to be a flood

11.
Weve had to call the plumber as the boilers on the blink
We aint got no hot water so were washing in the sink.

12.

The kazies got no water
The poo is rizing high
Little peter tells me, it's going to touch the sky

His mummy says don't use it son
You now must poo at grannies
You know the house its painted blue
Next door to uncle dannys.

13.
Harry is the plumber, he lives down by the docs
Youl always recognise him as he tends to where no socks
He dresses like a hippy and never looks the part
He stays out boozing all night long, then makes a latish start.

14.
Im looking for a plumber, iv serched around for ages
I should have been a clever chap and used the yellow pages

15.
Jack frosts out to freeze the pipes and make us all unhappy
Because he does this every year he is a roten chappie.
We try to make it hard for him and cover pipes with
lagging
But even after all our work we still can hear him laughing

16.
Plumbers from ireland, plumbers from wales
The irish are fast but the welsh are like snails
Plumbers from blighty far north of the tyne
Geordies are best, they win every time

17.

Im a tradesman off from work today, im in my chair relaxing
But as my wife is hoovering, she really is quite taxing
The noise is getting to my head, the dust is up my nose
If she don't stop this noise real soon, i think we,l come to
blows

18.
Some plumbers are fat, some plumbers are thin
Some work with a frown, some work with a grin
But show me a plumber who works fast and clean
And ill tell you that plumber has yet to be seen

19.
Plumbers in the basement, plumbers in the loft
Plumbers working hard all day, plumbers on the soft
Plumbers with a friendly smile, plumbers with a frown
Plumbersin the city rush, and plumbers in the town

Plumbers up in skeggie, plumbers up in leeds
Plumbers wearing thick gold rings, plumbers wearing beads
Plumbers with a crew-cut, plumbers going thin
Plumbers with a frosty look, plumbers with a grin

Plumbers sporting rood tatoos, displayed on both their arms
It always adds that little bit when turning on their charms

20.

Most plumbers vans are filthy and very seldome clean
Its not because their lazy chaps, its just because their mean
Too mean to buy a bucket with soap and mop and brush
As then theyd have to buy a pick to hack through all that
gunge
You see its not the owners fault, its normally the driver
Who,d rather wack it through the wash and give the guy a
fiver.

21.

I called a plumber late one night, his name was Kelso Mick
I said come quick, the sink is blocked, you see iv just been sick
He said ill charge you 50 quid, because it's after eight
And then another 20 quid, if i guess what you ate!.

22.

Plumbers working out on site in cold and wind and rain
Site work means the total job from taps, to pipe, to drain.
Its working up on scaffolding, and in a filthy trench
Oh how id rather be in bed and cuddling my wench

23.

P it is for plumber, a tradesman through and through
Wearing plumbers overalls quite often navy blue
Its bib and brace with leather belt and boots with leather laces
Great big chaps, with great big hands, and all unshaven faces

24.

My father was a plumber as was his dad before
And back they go through history, just breaking for the war
Wev kept it in the family, right up to present day
With faults a speciality, attended right away
We also do the big jobs, the hospital, the school
My father entertains the head, he really is no fool
He parts with wine and wisky at any time he can
That's why outside the grammer school, youl always see our
van

25.
Plumbers turning up on time, others rock up late
Plumbers working on their own, others with a mate

26.

Jimmy morris whent to hull to do a friend a favour
The friend said Jim it's worth a grand and Jim he didn't
waiver
He said im off, lets have the cash, i need to pour in diesel
Then of to number 26 to pick up my mate weasil
Jim and weasil hit the road with pipes and tool and taps
Off to do this little job, these two north country chaps
They hit the town at half past six, all tyred with distress
Then Jimmy said im such a nut ive come with no address

27.

Plumbers on a monday, rather slow and rough
Been drinking on a sunday night, far more than enough
Breath stinks like a brewewry wind at 20 knots
Ears with wax and eys with crust, and nose with hairs and
snots

28.

Some dads sons like rock and roll and long to be a
drummer
While some dads sons just want to work and strive to be a
plumber
Plumber drummer what the heck, they,l both make lots of
money
But only one has served his time, now isnt life quite funny

29.

Scottish plumber Tam Macdough wakes up fresh and frisky
Because he knows the more he makes, the more hell spend
on whisky
English plumber Kenny Kim, wakes up nice and merry
As many pounds as he can make, hell spend it all on sherry

30.
Irish plumber Phill Macavy, declairs iv strength withinus
For sure its cause im out each night, drinking pints of
guiness

31.

Taffy plumber Jones the tap, declairs im half asleep
That's as i was up all last night measuring my leak!

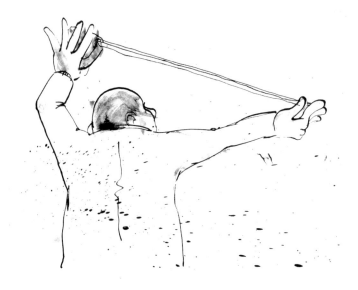

32.

Taffy was a tradesman working hard all day,

He,d worked his way from leaving school because that was the way

Hed studdied three years at the college, plus three years as an appy

Not for him the quick rush jobs where end results are crappy

His grandad and his father had handed down the firm

because of this, young tam he vowed to always graft and learn

To treat the publick nicelt as service never fails

Entrust to me your bursts and leaks, im taffy from south wales.

33.
Jack frosts frozen all the pipes, the temprature is zero
While mothrs nice and warm inside, baking cakes with
be-ro

34.
Water, water everywhere, and not a drop to drink
That's because it's dirty and sitting in the sink
The drain is blocked real solid with rice and old pea-pods
Looks like when my man comes home, hell have to get the rodds

35.

P is for plumber with bends and ball cock
L is for leaking with loud drips and drops
U is for u-bend fixed underthe sink
M is for mole-grip to tighten the link
B is for butt-gap that all plumbers show
E is for early when all plumbers go
R is for readys which all plumbers need
S is for salesmen, their families to feed

36.

Jones the plumber came to tea and sat right next to ma and me

We all sat round this one small table, jones the plumber me and mable

Mable is my mum you see, ive had no dad since i was three

He ran off with a real young stunner, and left my mum with jones the plumber

He sniffs around and brings her gifts, and when theres shopping, gives her lifts

Hed like his feet beneath our table, cause he likes mum, his dear old mable

37.
To find a plumber could take ages, local rag or yellow pages
Phone a friend or internet, they're under water, cold and
wet.

38.

Married to a plumber is such a lovely life, i fit into that
bracket i am a plumbers wife
We all live down in puddlecome, a village by the sea
We have two plumbers children, their names are bill and lee
We have a fair size garden where we keep some bees for
honey
My hubby bought this place for cash, as he makes lots of
money
He bought a little bike for bill, and then a horse for lee
Then on my birthday last weekend he bought a car for me

We go abroad three times a year to lovely sonny places
Then come back when we miss our friends with lovely sun
burnt faces
We go to movies and eat out, and really spend dads lolly
Go on, he says, you make me feel so jolly
So next time when you get your bill, don't waite two weeks
or three
Just draw the cash and pay the man, with many thanks from
me.

39.

Married plumbers, single plumbers, plumbers who are gay
Plumbers who where girlie shirts and say to "walk this way"
Plumbers who look mean and hard, and never shave for
days
And plumbers who sport rings and chains, because its all the
craze.

40.

I know a man called Dickie Mint who bought a house in stoke
It had no central heating, it really was no joke
He said it dosent matter, it's warm, as now it's summer
And when the winter nights come round, ill get myself a plumber
I know a place to get the parts, the total installation
Then Michael T will do the job, because he's my relation.

41.

There ws a joung plumber called Johnny who had a sweet daughter called Vonney
One night at the dance she tried some romance, now shes got her own baby Johnny.

42.

There once was a plumber called Ray, who's habit was always to stray

He,d set out for Leith, end up in Dalkeith and have to find somewhere to stay

43.

There was a young plumber called Jack, who fiddled and then got the sack

He said oh my gosh, ill now have no dosh, to the dole line ill have to go back

44.

Molly wed a plumber for better or for worst, she didn't get
her wedding night, the hotel had a burst
The manager he rang the room, and said this isnt funny, if
you come now and fix the pipe, well refund all your money
The plumber said ill do the job, but first ill get my brother,
with that his bride said sod you mate im going back to
mother

45.

If your looking for a plumber, you look in yellow pages, but
once you've rang and left your name he seems to take for
ages
He,l ring you when he,s readyor finished playing darts
if you've a burst or leaking roof, he couldn't give two farts

Don't get me wrong my readers i don't dislike the plumber,
Its just the fact he lets you down and that's the awfull
bummer
They charge you more than doctors, and give a shitty
service
That's why when frosty months come round, i start to get
real nervous.

46.

A plumber took a holiday upon a norfolk barge he could
have gone for single birth, but cash permitted large,
He took a really posh one, six berth was his wish,
It came with all the trimming, tv with a dish
A washer for the dishes, a hoover for the rugs,
An automatic sprayer for all those river bugs,
A microwave and toaster, and fridge to cool the drink
A fully hands-free mixer, that stood beside the sink

Strapped on top, a motorbike,that really made a noise
Next to that two scooters for both his little boys
The wife got loads of makeup, facials, gells and creams
And liz the girl got mills and boon for all those late night
dreams

47.

The plumber asked the stockist for some lengths of copper
pipe,
He said my sons a butcher can i pay the bill with tripe,
The stockist said of course you can, but just remember this,
my lad works down the sewage farm, your discounts paid
with p——.

48.

Plumber, plumber, fix my leak my tap has got an awfull
squeak
Iv bashed it and ive bonked it, and ive even fed it oil,
But every time i hear that drip, it makes my blood fair boil
It really isnt urgent, just come round when you can,
As im catching all the water in an old 5 gallon can.

49.
Mr plumber fix my loo, my hubby blocked it with his poo,
Youl need your rods and make it quick,
Before this odour makes me sick.

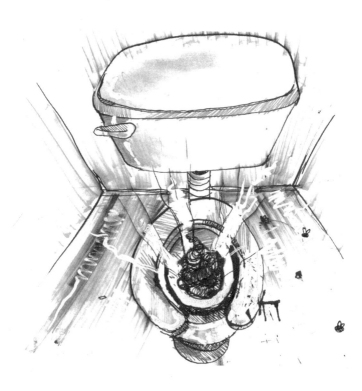

50.

I met a plumber late one night, he really gave me quite a fright
From this dark ally he did roll, disturbing my late evening stroll
He said im drunk, iv won the pools, ive sold my van and all my tools,
No more the business man am i, il live it up untill i die.

No more call ots, no more leaks, no more working 7 day weeks,
No more dull days, only sunny, as this ex plumbers in the money.
So join me for a happy drink, whats your name, mines geordie pink.

This book probably came about due to the many and varied short poems and limericks I would compose and send to my sweet Susan, she would always encourage me to "keep writing them, your not too bad, one day you could even have a book published" now 30 odd years down the line, guess what?.

I HAVE MY BOOK.

MY FAMILY

SARAH

NANCY

ME AND MY

INSPIRATION 1976

JOANNE

DICKIE

DAVID

HARRY

A SHORT VERSE FROM THE NEXT SERIES;

A BOOK OF LOVE POEMS.

You're beautiful; you're wonderful, just right in every way.

I worship you by stars above, from night till break of day.

You give me so much happiness, through thought and word and deed.

If you should ever leave me my heart would surely bleed.

To think it started with a smile, and now to man and wife.

You're gorgeous and I love you, for to me you are my life.

WHEN I THINK OF ALL THE MONEY I'VE
SPENT ON DRINKING AND HAVING FUN........
THANK GOODNESS I DIDN'T WASTE IT!.

David Weatherson